I BET I CAN/I BET YOU CAN'T

I BET I CAN
I BET YOU CAN'T

by
E. RICHARD CHURCHILL

ILLUSTRATIONS by
SANFORD HOFFMAN

Sterling Publishing Co., Inc. New York

For Mom who knows all the questions and most of the answers

Library of Congress Cataloging in Publication Data

Churchill, Elmer Richard.
I bet I can, I bet you can't.

Includes index.
1. Tricks—Juvenile literature. I. Hoffman, Sanford. II. Title.
GV1548.C45 1982 793.8 82-50551
ISBN 0-8069-4664-4
ISBN 0-8069-4665-2 (lib. bdg.)

Two Park Avenue, New York, N.Y. 10016
Distributed in Australia by Oak Tree Press Co., Ltd.
P.O. Box K514 Haymarket, Sydney 2000, N.S.W.
Distributed in the United Kingdom by Blandford Press
Link House, West Street, Poole, Dorset BH15 1LL, England
Distributed in Canada by Oak Tree Press Ltd.
% Canadian Manda Group, 215 Lakeshore Boulevard East
Toronto, Ontario M5A 3W9
Manufactured in the United States of America

CONTENTS

Before You Begin

We all like doing things that others can't do. Setting up friends and family and then fooling them is almost a national sport. That's what *I Bet I Can/I Bet You Can't* is all about. The tricks, stunts, and puzzles in this book are intended to give double enjoyment. Most of the items in *I Bet I Can/I Bet You Can't* are things for you to try first. Then, you get more fun when you dare others to do what you know how to do. Or, you can dare others to try something, which looks easy, but which you now know is impossible. Either way, you are the winner since you've gotten double the fun.

The first part of the book is called "Let's Get Physical." The stunts and problems in this part all require some sort of physical action. The action may be as simple as dropping a card or as difficult as standing next to a wall. Some of the stunts are impossible. Others are pretty easy to do once you learn the way. In some cases a solution is placed upside down at the bottom of the page. And, of course, after you have tried the impossible stunt or figured out the other trick, it is time for you to present the dare to your friends and family.

In the next part, "Make Your Move," you are given a variety of tricks and puzzles which require a few coins, some pieces of paper, a pencil, and such. All of these stunts are based on moving things from place to place or on deciding where to put things. Some can't be done even though they seem too simple to even bother with. Others may appear difficult, though they turn out to be fairly simple once you have learned how to do the stunt. Again, you will be told if a problem is impossible.

The final part is "Listen as You Look." Most of the stunts in this part are for you to read over, see how the trick works, then present to others. A few ask you to figure out the stunt before trying it on your friends and other victims. Answers to these are given. Simple as the tricks in this part seem, you will be surprised how many times you can trip up even your sharpest friends.

Try the stunts in *I Bet I Can/I Bet You Can't*, first. Be sure you understand the rules of each problem before you present them as dares to others.

LET'S GET PHYSICAL

Act Like a Flamingo

Flamingos are those pinkish birds you see in zoos. One interesting thing about flamingos is that so many of them stand around on one leg.

Is there any place in the room you can't stand on one leg for as long as five seconds? There is.

Stand with one side against the wall. Be sure your shoulder and the side of your foot touch the wall. Now lift the other foot from the floor and try to remain standing. Try is all you can do. You'll find you can't remain standing in this position no matter how hard you work at it.

After you're sure that this is impossible, it is time to go in search of victims. Issue your dare by saying, "I bet I can find a place in this room where you can't stand on one leg!"

When your dare is accepted, do your stuff. You've just made a sure bet.

Trapped by a Bottleneck

Place a soft-drink bottle upside down on a dollar bill as shown below. As you can see, the bottle has the dollar trapped under it.

All you need do to meet the dare is remove the dollar bill from under the bottle without tipping the bottle over. Don't touch the bottle. Don't pick it up. Don't hold it steady. Don't brace anything against the bottle to steady it. Just remove the dollar without tipping, moving, or touching the bottle.

If this one stumps you, check the upside-down answer. Don't give up too soon. It is a lot easier than it looks at first glance.

Turn page upside down for answer.

Roll one end of the dollar bill tightly around a pencil. Keep rolling the pencil toward the bottle. The bill will slowly slide from under the bottle, leaving the bottle standing.

Magic Match

Did you ever stop to think how many tricks and stunts depend upon wooden matches to make them work? Well, here's another.

Break a *used* wooden match in half as shown here. Do not break it into two pieces. Be sure the match is still held together by the fibres along one side of the match.

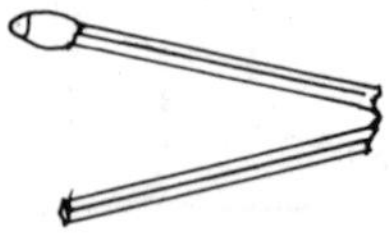

Place the broken match carefully on the table in front of your future victim. Tell him or her, "I bet I can make this match move. I won't hit the table. I won't blow on the match. I won't push the match with a stick or any such thing. But in spite of the fact that I won't touch the match or the table, I can make the match move."

After your victim has asked you about a number of possible tricks, he or she will probably accept your dare.

Use a spoon or even your fingers to bring a drop of water to the table above the match. Drop just one drop of water onto the broken part of the match. As the wood in the match swells from the water, the match will begin to open slightly, using the broken spot as a hinge.

Try it on your own just to prove to yourself that this trick really works. (And remember, don't play with any matches unless they have already been used!)

Easy Money

Everyone likes a chance to earn some easy money. Here is a stunt, which looks like a quick way to pick up a coin, but isn't.

Have your victim stand with his heels against the wall. Place a coin on the floor about two feet in front of your friend's toes.

Tell your friend to pick up the coin without moving his heels away from the wall. Also, tell him he cannot lift his heels from the floor.

As easy as this seems, it is impossible to do. By keeping one's heels on the floor and against the wall, it is physically impossible to bend over or kneel down to pick up the coin.

Try this stunt several times yourself before daring others to try it.

Don't Fold Up

When you say, "I bet you can't fold a piece of paper in half ten times," you're almost sure to get an answer to your dare.

The rules are simple: Your opponent picks any piece of paper he or she wishes. It may be as large or as small, as thick or as thin, as he or she wants. The rules are as easy to understand. Fold the paper in half. Then fold it again in half. Then again and again and again. Each fold must make the paper half the size it was before the fold.

Folds may be horizontal or vertical. They may even be diagonal if the folder wishes. It does not matter.

What does matter is that no matter the size or thickness of the paper, no one, *but no one,* is ever going to be able to fold it the tenth time.

Try it yourself just to be sure.

That Tears It

While your victim watches you closely, make two tears in a piece of paper. This leaves the paper looking something like this.

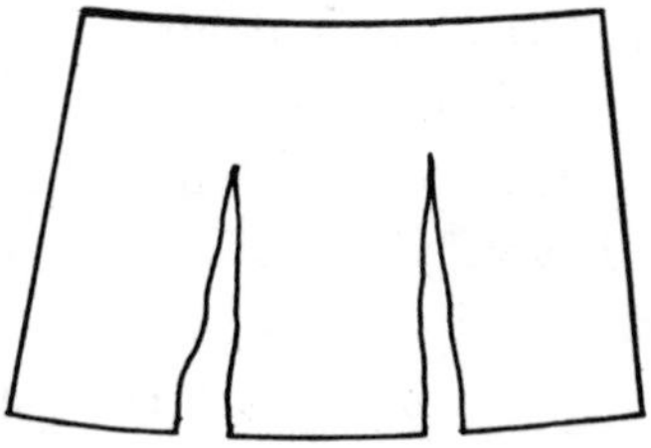

Give your victim your best smile and say, "I bet you can't take hold of one end of the paper in each hand and tear off both ends in one quick pull."

Your victim will probably look at the tears, and, since they are the same length, take you up on it.

You'll win every time. Only one end will tear free. Try it yourself just to be sure.

Sunken Treasure

If you have a steady hand and a bit of patience, this stunt should be right up your alley. Begin by filling a glass with water to the brim. Next, you need a handful of pennies. Dimes will do fine, but pennies are easier to get.

The question is: How many pennies can you drop into the glass without having the water run over? Remember, the glass is already full of water. Can you drop in one penny before the glass runs over? How about two? Five? Ten? How many?

Try it, and you will be more than a little surprised. Drop the pennies one at a time. Wait until one penny has settled to the bottom of the glass before dropping the next one. Drop the pennies as gently as possible. Let the surface of the water become calm before dropping the next penny. Be careful not to touch the water with your fingers when dropping the pennies.

As more and more pennies go into the glass full of water an interesting thing happens. The water will actually begin to rise above the edge of the glass. Eventually you will be able to see the water standing higher than the glass which is holding it. This has to do with what is called the *surface tension* of the water.

There is no exact limit to the number of pennies you can drop into a full glass of water. It depends upon the size of the glass, among other things. Don't be surprised if you run out of pennies before the water runs over!

When you have practiced a few times, you should be ready to go in search of a victim. Show the person the full glass of water and your handful of pennies. Say something like, "I bet I can drop all these pennies into that glass of water without having the water run over."

When your victim says, "No way!" or something of the sort, you're ready to once again prove you can do what seems impossible.

If you really get into this stunt, you might want to try dropping straight pins into the water instead of pennies. If you do, just be sure you have lots and lots of time, pins, and patience.

Hanging by a Thread

To get the attention of your victim, take a piece of string a couple of feet long and tie one end of it around a pen or pencil. Tie the other end of the string into a loop and let your friend hold it. Now, you are set for action.

"I bet I can cut the string you are holding, and the pen stays hanging in air," you claim. Go on to say, "I won't try to catch it after I cut the string. I'll cut the string about halfway between the pen and your hand. After I cut the string, I won't touch it."

This will be too much for your friend to believe. Then, it is time for you to prove you are correct.

First, tie a loop and knot in the middle of the string as shown in the drawing. Now, cut the string in the middle of the loop.

The pen or pencil will not fall. You will have won. Your victim will go in search of a victim of his or her own, and a new stunt will have started.

Four from Four Leaves Eight

Hand a square or rectangular sheet of paper to a friend. Give him or her a pencil as well.

"I bet I can take four from four and leave eight," you tell your friend. "See whether or not you can. If you can't, then I'll show you how it is done."

Of course your friend will try all sorts of solutions. Roman numerals are usually tried. Fractions are another good bet. Unless your friend comes up with some fancy math as yet unknown, there isn't a chance in the world that your friend can come up with an answer to this stumper.

When your friend gives up, it is time for you to shine. Take the paper and show your friend it has four corners. Tear each corner off as shown below.

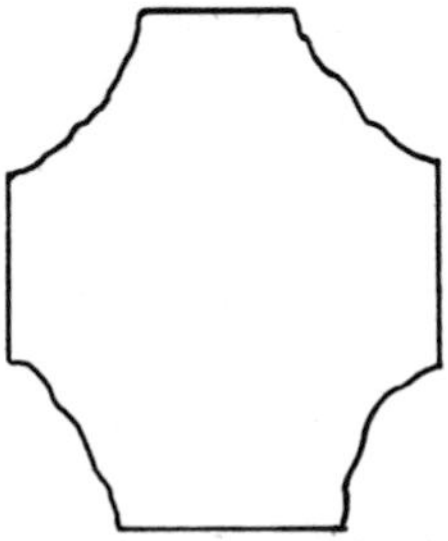

While your friend is still sputtering say, "There were four corners. I took those four corners away. Now there are eight corners left on the paper."

It is probably best that you not say anything more at this time. Chances are you've said all that needs saying.

Money Slips Away

Did you ever notice how easily money gets away from you? It is almost like having a hole in your pocket. This problem may help show how easily money slips away.

Begin with a sheet of paper. It doesn't have to be a very big sheet. Place a dime flat on the paper. Draw around the dime. Then carefully cut out the circle you just drew. You now have a piece of paper which looks something like this.

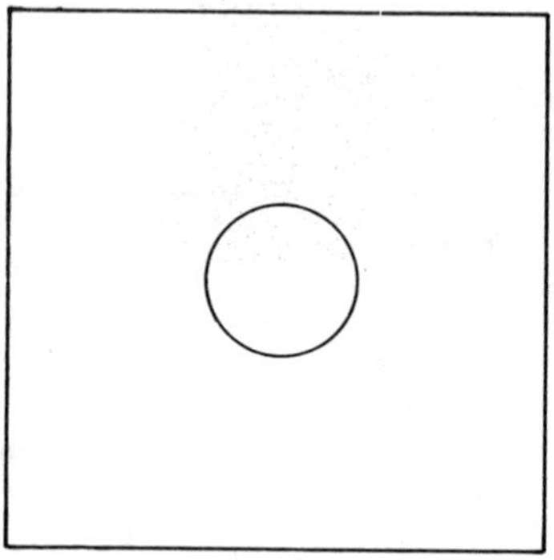

Now for the dare. You are going to push a quarter through the hole you just cut, and do it without tearing or ruining the paper. Give it some thought and try possible ways of doing this. You should be able to find the solution on your own. If not, or if you wish to check your solution, turn the next page upside down, and see how this stunt can be done.

Then you're ready to go looking for people to accept your bet when you show them a dime-sized hole and say, "I bet I can put a quarter through this hole without ripping the paper!"

Turn page upside down for answer.

Fold and crease the paper so that it looks like this.

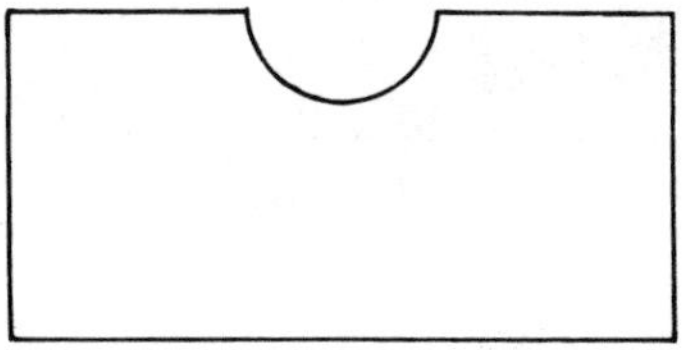

Drop the quarter inside the folded paper and gently work the ends of the folded paper upwards. The quarter will slip through the hole.

Hands Down

Here is just the thing for those big tough guys who think they can do anything. Before showing this stunt to anyone else though, try it yourself.

Begin by placing your hand on a table so that the fleshy part of the thumb, forefinger, ring finger, and little finger press down. Bend the middle finger back so that the finger joint rests firmly on the tabletop as well.

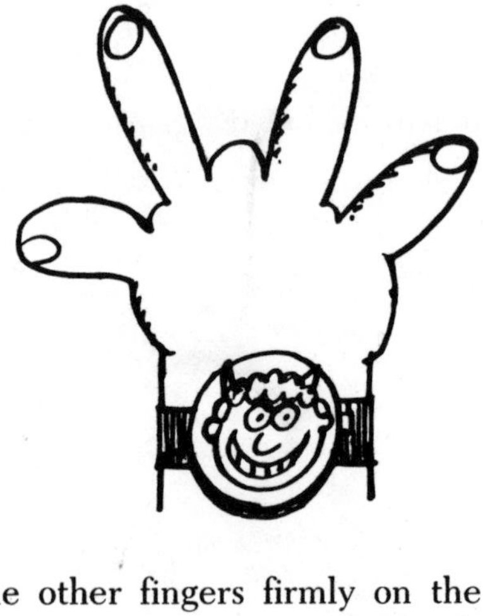

Keeping the other fingers firmly on the table, lift your thumb an inch or so from the tabletop. Return it to its position. Lift the forefinger an inch and return it. Do the same with your little finger. Nothing to it, is there?

Now, with the thumb and other fingers firmly on the table, try to lift your ring finger from the top of the table.

It can't be done! So long as the joint of the middle finger and the thumb and other fingers touch the table, you simply can't lift the tip of your ring finger from the top of the table.

Don't strain and struggle trying to lift the ring finger because you might make your hand sore if you try too hard for too long a time.

Now that you have found how impossible this stunt is, you're ready to try it on your friends. Watch the surprised looks on their faces as people try to do what *seems* very easy but *is* impossible.

Blow by Blow

Put a Ping-Pong ball on a table. Blow steadily on it and watch it roll away from you. When everyone is convinced it is an ordinary ball, you can make your dare.

Put the ball in a kitchen funnel. Hold the funnel so the wide mouth is up, and the small opening points down.

Tell your listeners, "I bet that, blowing steadily, no one here can blow this ball up and out of the mouth of the funnel."

Naturally, such an easy task gets lots of takers. It also causes lots of anger. No matter how hard a person blows upward through the funnel, the ball won't fly out of the funnel. It spins and turns and even hops around a bit, but it stays in the funnel through even the windiest of blows.

Here's a warning. Don't let players blow in short spurts. Make it clear they may blow as hard and as long as they wish, but they must blow a steady stream of air into the funnel.

It seems so easy but is impossible. Try it and see.

Hands Off

Here's one that is so easy it looks hard. Place any item in your right hand. A coin, a toy, a book, anything is just fine. Stand with your arms stretched straight out and apart as shown here.

With both arms still outstretched, move the object from your right hand to your left. Do it without bending your elbows. Don't bring your arms together. Don't bend your wrists.

Above all, don't give up too quickly. It is really quite easy once you figure it out. If you can't, the solution is upside down below.

Turn page upside down for answer.

Place the object on a table or counter. Then, with your arms still straight, turn halfway around and pick up the object with your other hand.

For Windy Characters

Blow up a balloon so that others see you do it. Then let the air out. Push the balloon into the mouth of a soft-drink bottle. Stretch the balloon's opening over the mouth of the bottle. Let everyone see exactly what you are doing.

Tell the others, "I bet no one can blow up the balloon so that it fills the bottle."

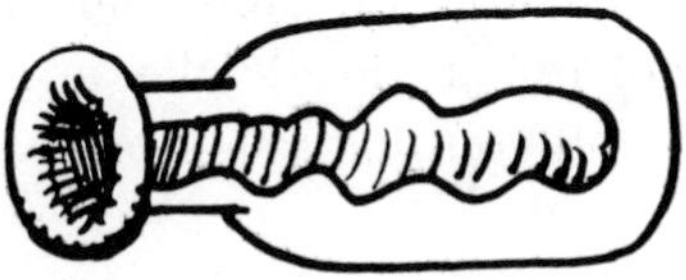

Since everyone just saw you blow up the balloon, and the bottle is so small, it looks like an easy bet to win. It is. For you.

Others may huff and puff but they simply can't blow up the balloon to the point it fills the inside of the bottle. With every bit the balloon expands, it gets harder and harder to blow up.

There is no trick to it. Your victims can't blow up the balloon in the bottle. You can't. It is a matter of air pressure. Though it looks easy, the balloon in the bottle is a match for anyone.

By a Waterfall

Fill a glass full of water to the brim. Over the top of the glass, place a small piece of thin cardboard. (A chunk cut from a file folder is perfect.)

Now for the dare. Suggest that you plan to turn the filled glass upside down while holding the cardboard in place. Add that you will then take your hand away from the cardboard. When you do this, tell your friend that you think the water will remain inside the upside-down glass.

Your victim may tell you that you'll be making a waterfall instead!

If you do the stunt carefully, you'll be a sure winner. But first, a warning. Practice this over the kitchen sink several times. Be sure the glass is completely full to the brim. Also be sure the cardboard is sealed tightly when you turn the glass over. Finally, take your hand away from the cardboard very slowly once you have the glass upside down.

What is called *atmospheric pressure* will hold the cardboard in place since the weight of the air pushing up is greater than the weight of the water pushing down. This is true, however, only so long as you don't let the cardboard pull away from the rim of the glass before you let go of the cardboard.

Lead Foot

It is upsetting to find out that you cannot do even the simplest things from time to time. Well, here's another of those simple things, which is impossible.

Tell your victim you will make it impossible for him or her to jump even a few inches off the floor. Promise you won't touch the person. You'll allow him or her to stand alone and not have to hold onto anything heavy.

Of course there is one little catch. The person, trying to jump, must stand with his or her back to a wall. The victim's heels, hips, and shoulders must touch the wall. Then, without bending or leaning forward, the victim must try to jump.

It isn't possible in the position just described. Try it a few times yourself just to make certain. Then go looking for someone who is willing to accept your dare.

It's a Toss-up

Remove a paper match from a match book. Carefully tear the head from the match and throw the head away. Show the match.

Tell your victim, "I bet if I toss this match into the air it will land on its edge on the table. If it lands on either side you win. If it lands on either edge I win."

Most people will accept your bet. If your opponent wants to check the match by tossing it a few times, that's fine. However, when the bet is made you must be the one to toss the match into the air.

You'll win. Can you figure out how to make sure you win? If you can't, turn the page upside-down.

Turn page upside down for answer.

Bend the match in half just before you toss it up. This will cause it to land on its edge.

A Difficult Burden

You can play this as a quick bet you'll always win or spend a lot of time giving it a big buildup. Either way you will have a winning stunt.

It goes like this: "I bet I can have you hold something in your right hand which you can't hold in your left no matter how strong you are."

Of course you can draw things out by talking about a newspaper article you just read which explains that people can hold much more weight in one hand than in another. You may even go into a long story about possible reasons people can hold more weight in their right hand than in their left. That's up to you.

At any rate, once your dare has been accepted, take the person's right hand in yours and place it beneath his or her left elbow.

You can then say, "You are now holding your left elbow in your right hand. Can you hold your left elbow in your left hand?"

It's impossible, of course, and you've won.

It Has to Be Magic

Here is a stunt that you will enjoy doing over and over. Begin by folding a dollar bill into the shape of an S as shown below.

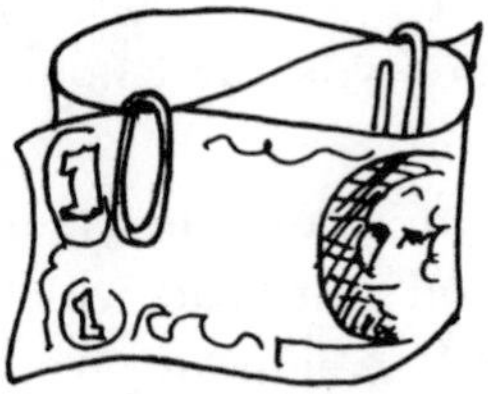

Hook the short, single side of one paper clip over two thicknesses of the dollar bill as shown in the drawing. Then hook the short wire of a second paper clip over the other two thicknesses of the bill.

Once your victim sees what you are doing, it is time to make your bet. You can say something such as, "I bet I can hook these two paper clips together without touching them. I'll just pull the bill away from them, and they will be hooked due to my magic powers."

Who can resist a bet like that? Once you've "gotten your victim on the hook," grasp each end of the bill firmly. Then, with a quick snap, pull the two ends of the bill in opposite directions. Of course the bill will straighten out. But something else happens at the same time. The two paper clips fly off the bill. And guess what? They are hooked together! Try it and find out for yourself.

Sit This One Out

You don't have to rehearse this stunt to get it right the first time. Just tell someone, "I bet I can find a place to sit in this room where I can sit, but you can't."

Who can turn down a dare like that?

First, you sit in a chair.

After you get up, your victim sits in the same chair.

Next, you might sit on the floor.

Your victim will sit on the floor exactly where you sat.

This can go on for as long as you wish to stretch out the stunt.

Finally, have your victim sit in a chair, on a sofa, or wherever you wish. When your victim is seated, you sit in the person's lap.

There shouldn't be a bit of doubt but that you have won your bet. If there is any question, dare the victim to sit in his or her own lap. It can't be done.

Five Sure Bets

See whether you can figure out how to win each of the following bets. After you've seen through each bet or given up and checked the answer, you're ready to add five more surefire bets to your collection of ways to triumph over friends and foes alike.

Bet 1. Tell your opponent, "I bet I can write a longer word than you."

Most people will search their minds and, perhaps, the dictionary for long words. No matter what they write, you will win your bet. Reread the bet and decide how this can be so.

Bet 2. For this one, you need a deck of cards. Hand the deck to your victim. Tell this lucky person, "I bet I can hand you any card from the deck which you select. You

may shuffle the deck as many times as you wish. All I ask is that you keep thinking of the card you have chosen."

No matter how carefully your victim shuffles the deck, you will always be able to hand him or her the proper card. Do you see how to win this bet?

Bet 3. Here's a bet with a solution so simple it is almost impossible to figure out for most people. Just tell someone, "I bet I can drop a spoonful of sugar (or a lump of sugar) into a cup of coffee without getting the sugar wet."

No, you don't wrap the sugar in plastic! Can you see through this bet?

Bet 4. Tell a friend, "I bet I can show you something you have never seen before. After I show it to you, you will never be able to see it again."

This sounds so unlikely most people will take you up on your bet. Of course, you win the bet. But don't you nearly always win?

Bet 5. Have someone write six or eight words on a piece of paper. Make sure he or she does this in such a way that there is no chance that you will see what is written on the paper. Then ask the person to fold the paper two or three times so the words are completely hidden from view. Last, but certainly most important, have your victim place the paper on the floor and cover it with one foot.

Now say, "In spite of all the precautions you have taken, I bet I can tell you what is on that paper." And of course you can! Every time you find a victim, you'll win this bet.

Turn page upside down for answers.

Bet 1. Write "a longer word than you."

Bet 2. Hand your victim the entire deck of cards. You've handed him the card he chose.

Bet 3. Drop the sugar into a cup of dry coffee.

Bet 4. Crack a nut. Show the others the nut from inside the shell. Eat the nut.

Bet 5. Tell your victim his or her foot is on the paper. It is.

Bottoms Up

This is a good one for a hot summer day but it works well at any time.

Pick up a glass containing water, iced tea, soda, or whatever you are drinking. (A can or bottle of soft drink works just as well.)

Study the container of liquid. Then finger the material of your shirt or blouse.

When you have everyone's attention, it is time to tell them, "I bet I can pour this water (or whatever) down my neck without getting my shirt wet."

It seems like a good idea to others even if the only gain is seeing you making a mess.

When the dare has been agreed upon, all you have to do to win is to drink whatever is in the container. You've poured it down your neck, haven't you? And unless someone tries to drown you for setting them up, your shirt won't be even damp from your efforts.

There's a Trick to It

Are you up to what seems an impossible problem, but which has an obvious answer? If so, this one is for you. Just look for the trick which makes it all possible.

Place a quarter on a table. Place a penny beside it on the table. The object of the stunt is to place the penny under the quarter. You may touch the penny. You may not touch the quarter in any way, shape, or form. Do not use anything such as a piece of paper to move the quarter. It must be left exactly as it is.

When you figure this one out, check the upside-down answer at the bottom of the page. Then go looking for someone to be your victim when you bet them you can place the penny under the quarter without touching the quarter or even moving it.

Turn page upside down for answer.

Pick up the penny and hold it under the table beneath the quarter. The penny is now under the quarter.

Magic Yardstick

Stick out your index fingers and place a yardstick on them so that one index finger is at either end of the yardstick. Then very slowly begin to move your fingers toward each other. First one finger will move and then the other. No matter which finger moves along the yardstick first, nor for how far, both fingers will eventually meet in the middle of the yardstick. Remember! Move your fingers slowly with this stunt.

Once your fingers are together near the middle of the yardstick, begin slowly moving them apart. Surprise! One finger moves and the other stays right about where it was.

No matter how many times you repeat this stunt, the same thing will always happen. When coming together, your fingers meet in the middle. When pulling apart from the center, one finger moves while the other stays in place.

Try this one a few times. Then let others try it. So long as the fingers are moved slowly you can bet on the outcome and always be right.

Stand Firm

People admire those who take a firm stand on issues. With this stunt you can take a firm stand on a piece of paper.

Drop a sheet of paper on the floor and announce, "I bet I can stand on this paper in such a way that nobody can push me off."

Naturally a dare of that sort can't go unanswered. When someone accepts it, be sure everyone understands the rules.

Tell the group you will place the paper at a point of your choice. Only one opponent at a time may challenge you. Each of you will stand with at least one foot on the paper. In order to win, all you have to do is stand firm and not be pushed or pulled from the paper by your opponent. And

finally, your opponent may touch only you in pushing you from the paper. He or she may not touch another object which in turn touches or pushes you from the paper.

When the rules are agreed upon, you are on your way to winning. Place the paper in the middle of a doorway. Be sure the door opens into the room in which you will stand. Have your opponent stand on the end of the paper on one side of the doorway. Close the door. Then you stand on that part of the paper which extends into the room beneath the closed door.

There isn't a way in the world your opponent can push or pull you from the paper!

An Impossible Test of Strength

At one time or another all of us have met the person who is just *too* perfect. This is the one who makes all the teams, wins in every sport, and who is as strong as an ox. Or, there is the person who boasts and brags until it is almost impossible to tell what is the truth and what is made up. This test of strength has been designed just for the person with Superman strength or the person who never seems to stop bragging about him- or herself.

Fill a glass nearly full of water. Again, a plastic glass is better to use than one made of real glass. Go up to your victim with the glass of water balanced on the palm of your hand. Hold your arm straight out with the water glass in hand.

Tell Superkid, "I bet you can't hold this glass of water in the palm of your hand with your arm straight out from your shoulder just as mine now is. At least you can't do it for more than just a few minutes."

Now who can turn down a challenge like that? Certainly not Superkid. Try to get your victim to set the amount of time he or she will hold the glass. The longer the better. Five minutes is great. Seven or eight minutes are even better. Be sure the arm is extended straight out from the shoulder. Don't allow the victim to bend his or her elbow while holding the glass. After a couple of minutes you'll be able to see the strain. Most people give up long before five minutes pass. No one ever lasts as much as seven or eight minutes. (If you run into a victim who does survive that long, the chances are you've just run into the world's next champion something or other!)

Even when not used as a putdown, this is a good stunt. It looks easy but quickly proves otherwise. Don't be surprised when a slender cheerleader holds the glass longer than Mr. Muscles from the football team. It can happen just that way.

Don't Hang Up

For this puzzler you need a cup and a piece of string about four feet long. Don't use one of your mother's best china cups for this stunt. A plastic unbreakable cup is far better in case things go wrong.

Double the string so that it is now two feet long with a loop in one end. Place the loop through the cup's handle and thread the loose ends of the string through the loop. Tie the loose ends to a hook, a door knob, a cupboard handle, or what have you.

Now for the challenge. Can you remove the cup from the string without cutting the string, unfastening the string from where it is tied, or breaking the cup?

Try it. It is not at all hard.

When you bet people you can do this stunt, don't let them handle the cup or the string. Let them look at it without trying it for themselves. Then show them you can win yet another bet.

Turn page upside down for answer.

Just pull the center of the loop upward until you've made the loop bigger than the cup. Pass the cup through the enlarged loop and the cup is free. Don't drop it.

That's the Date

Have someone place a coin on the table with the head side of the coin up. Then tell them to put a piece of blank paper over the coin.

You're then ready to make your bet. "I bet I can tell you the date on that coin without touching the coin and without lifting or removing the paper from the coin," you say.

It looks impossible. Chances are someone will take you up on your bet. You'll win, naturally.

How? Here's a hint. You need a soft lead pencil to help you along.

After you've checked the upside-down answer on this stunt to see how it is done, here's another hint. Practice this stunt several times before trying it on others. It does take a bit of care in order to work properly.

Turn page upside down for solution.

Use a soft lead pencil to color over the paper which is on top of the coin. Don't let the paper slip while doing this. The coin's date will appear plainly on the paper you are blacking in with pencil lead.

MAKE YOUR MOVE

Just Do What I Do

Place three glasses on a table as shown below. The object of the stunt (your part of it, that is) is to turn two glasses over at a time. Do this three times and end with all three glasses standing so the open part of each glass faces up. While you make the three moves necessary to do this, tell your victim to watch your moves carefully.

Try this stunt a time or two until you're sure you can do it in three moves. The moves are in the upside-down answer, but you shouldn't need them.

After you've made the three moves, it is time to say to your victim, "I bet you can't do what I just did in three moves. Remember you may turn two and only two glasses over in each move. You can take only three moves, and when you complete the third move, all three glasses must be standing with their open ends up."

It's a strange thing, but no matter how carefully your victim watched at the end of his or her three moves, the three glasses won't be standing with their open ends up. The upside-down answer tells why.

Turn page upside down for answer.

One way to solve the first step is to turn over glasses 2 and 3, then turn over 1 and 3, and finally turn over 2 and 3.

When you set the glasses up for your opponent, you do something sneaky. You set them up so that the two end glasses have their open ends up and the middle glass has the opening down. If you do this, few people will catch on. The difference makes it impossible to turn all three glasses open-end-up in three moves. Try it for yourself.

Last One Loses

This game has been played for years and years. It looks simple and is. However, it makes a great trick once you know the secret. Begin by making sixteen marks on a piece of paper or a blackboard so they look like this.

The object of the game is to remove either one, two, or three marks at a time. Players take turns, of course. The player who crosses off the last mark loses.

Naturally, there is a way to change this from a game of luck into a contest of skill. To do so, make sure you always leave your opponent with thirteen, nine, five, and then one marks to remove. It is that simple. Just remember the numbers 13, 9, 5, and 1.

If you go first, you can always win. Just take away three marks and then, no matter what your opponent takes, take enough to leave him or her with nine. Then leave your victim with five and no matter what he or she does, you can arrange things so your opponent has to cross off the last mark.

When your opponent begins play, just keep the numbers 13, 9, 5, and 1 in mind. Do your best to leave the other player facing these numbers. Once you can do this, you can carry on and win.

Use Your Head

Begin by setting up six coins in a row as shown below. The first three are heads up. The other three coins are tails up.

Here is the problem. You must move the coins around so that every other coin is heads. The coins will be head, tail, head, tail, head, and tail.

When making changes, you must turn over two coins each time. The coins you turn over have to be side-by-side. Each move, then, means turning over any two coins which are next to each other.

You can solve the problem in three moves.

After working it out, check your system with the upside-down answer.

When sure of yourself, show this problem to others, and see how long it takes them to solve it. Some will try it a few times and tell you it is impossible. At that point you can say, "I bet I can do it," then prove that you can.

Turn page upside down for answer.

Turn over coins 3 and 4. Then turn over 4 and 5. Finally turn over 2 and 3.

Be Quick About It

This stunt which requires changing the order of things is another of those which lots and lots of people make much harder than it is.

Begin by setting up six glasses as shown below. The first three glasses contain water. The next three are empty.

The trick is to move the six glasses around so that every other one is full. In other words. put the six glasses in a new order so that the first glass is full, the second is empty, the third is full, and so on.

Now, here's the catch. Do this in the least possible number of moves. Count it as a move each time you touch a glass or change its position. Take enough time to think this problem through before making your first move. You may want to try it a number of times just to be certain you are making the change in the least possible number of moves.

When you are sure you've done it, check the answer below.

After you've checked the answer you are ready to dare others to a contest. Explain the object of the puzzle. Dare them to make the change in fewer moves than you. This is a contest you can't lose. A very, very few people may be able to make the change in the same number of moves as you do. No one will ever make it in less! That's a promise.

Turn page upside down for answer.

Pour the second glass into the fifth in one move.

The Doors Are Open

On this page you see the floor plan of a strange building. The building, in fact, is a prison. It was built by a judge with a very odd sense of humor.

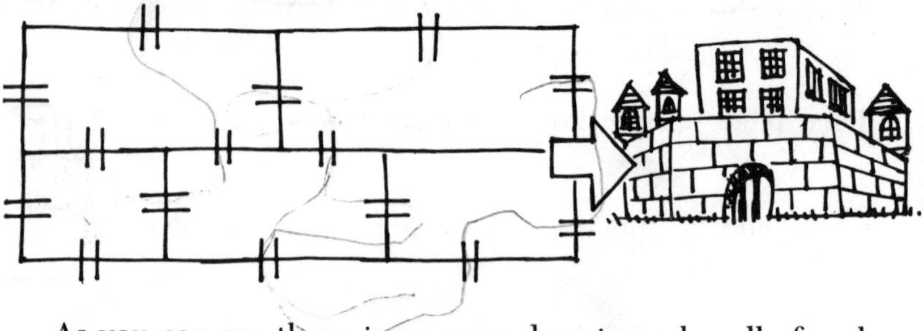

As you can see there is an open door in each wall of each room. (Some rooms actually have two doors in one wall due to the way the prison is built.)

The judge offered each newly convicted prisoner his or her freedom if they could do one thing. The one thing was easy enough. All the prisoner had to do was to start anywhere either inside or outside the prison building. From the starting point the prisoner merely had to go through each door in the prison one time and one time only. Any prisoner who did this was too smart to be in prison and would be released immediately.

As we said, the judge had a strange sense of humor. Since no prisoner ever completed the task, the judge never let anyone out of prison. By now you are saying you could have gotten out. You couldn't. The judge knew this task was impossible. It can't be done.

Even so, you will want to try. Start at any point. Go through each door one time and once only. Do not try to go through the walls. Just go through the doors. It cannot be done. But you will have to experiment to prove it to yourself.

Many people think they have accomplished the task. They haven't. In every case they either go through a door twice, skip a door, or go through the wall. Or, in drawing the prison, they forget to put in one door or put in one extra. Watch for these mistakes when you bet someone they can't get out of prison even with all the doors wide open.

Not Just For Squares

Everybody is always looking for a trick which can be done easily. This one should fill the bill.

Draw a square. Inside the square, draw four straight lines. Each line should extend from one side of the square to another side.

The trick is to divide the square into as many pieces as possible by drawing the four straight lines.

Here's a hint to get you started. The answer is more than eight. So keep trying until you are sure you've done it. Then, and only then, should you check the answer to see how well you have really done.

When you make this dare to others, you are usually on pretty safe ground. Not many people see the right answer without giving the square quite a bit of study.

Turn page upside down for answer.

Eleven pieces is the best possible effort. Do it like this.

Spelling Lesson

Study the jumble of letters below.

A D O O N Y E R W O O E N D N L N

Move them so they spell one word and only one.

Don't worry about words you have never heard of. Don't bother trying to think of people's names, of foreign countries, or of other strange and wonderful words and names.

Just stick to common words and you'll do fine.

If you get stuck, and many do, the answer is upside down on this page.

Whether you have to check the answer or find it on your own, this is a good one to use on the person who is a whiz at spelling and who never makes a mistake.

Turn page upside down for answer.

Sort the letters so they spell ONE WORD AND ONLY ONE.

One, Two, Three, Four

To get the attention of the people you want to confuse with this trick, begin by putting a cup on a table and slowly dropping four pennies into it. After dropping the pennies one at a time into the cup, you're bound to have the interest and attention of all.

Pour the four pennies from the cup into your hand and make your bet. "I bet I can drop these four pennies one at a time into that cup. Then I bet I can pick them up again, one at a time, and when I've picked up all four I'll still have one penny in the cup."

That sounds so impossible that someone will take you up on it.

Slowly drop the pennies into the cup, one at a time.

Then take one penny from the cup.

Say, "As you can see, I've picked up one penny."

Take the second penny and tell the group.

Do the same for the third penny.

Then pick up the cup with the fourth penny still inside.

"See," you tell the group. "I just picked up the fourth and final penny, and it's still in the cup."

Better not expect great applause. You probably won't receive many cheers, but you've won.

Upsy Daisy

Arrange ten coins so they look like this. (Or, make ten circles on a piece of paper.)

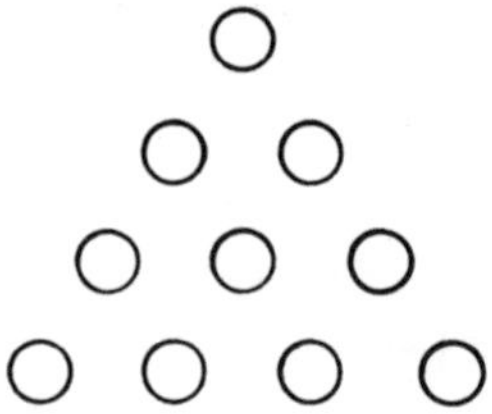

Now for the dare. Move three of the coins and only three. (Or, erase three circles and draw them in a new place.) After having moved the three coins you will have turned the pattern upside down so that it now looks like this.

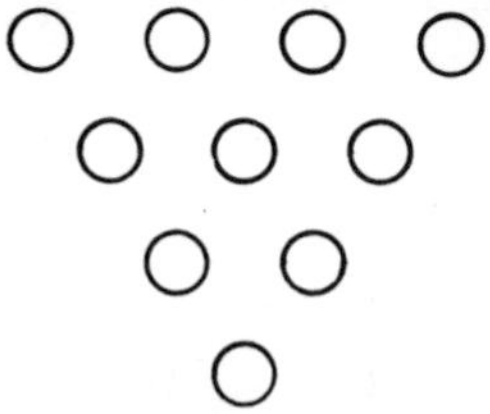

It is not all that difficult but neither is it terribly easy. If you get totally stuck or just want to check your answer, the solution is upside down.

When you have mastered this reversal it is time to challenge a friend to reverse the coin pattern by just moving three of the coins.

Turn page upside down for answer.

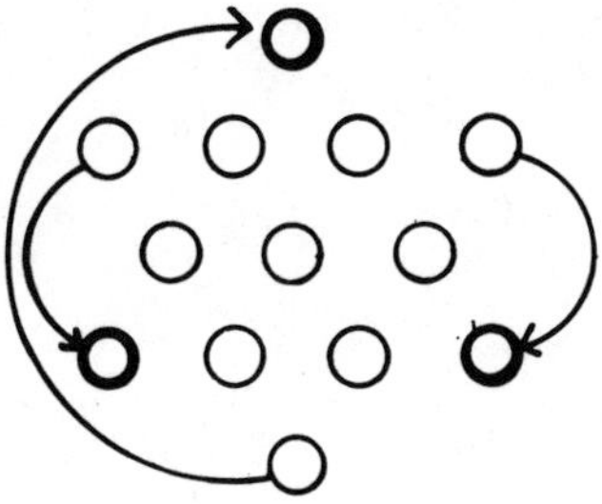

Move the three coins to the new positions as shown by the arrows.

Drive Them Dotty

Draw the group of dots shown below on a piece of paper. Dare a friend to connect all nine by drawing five straight lines and not lifting the pencil from the paper once the drawing begins. Begin at any point but do the connecting with only five straight lines.

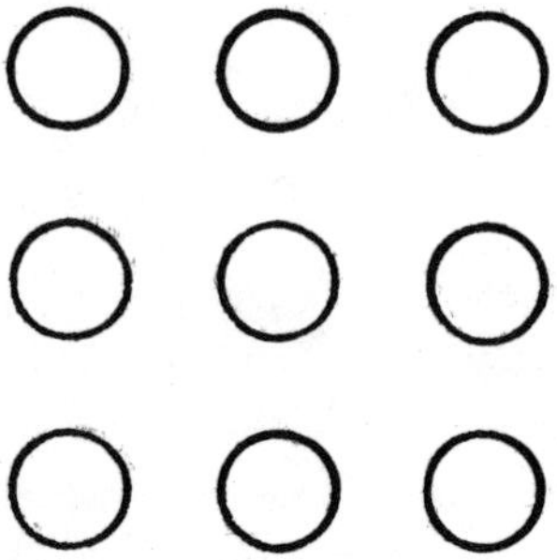

Of course your friend can do this in an instant. It is almost too easy to be worth doing.

While your friend is still basking in the warm glow of success, make your bet.

Tell your successful friend, "I'll bet you can't connect the same set of dots without raising your pencil from the paper and by drawing only four straight lines this time. What's more, I bet I can."

Who can turn down an easy dare like that? Especially after just having met your first dare, it is all but impossible to turn down.

Try doing this in both five and in four moves before looking for victims. Answers for both are upside-down.

Turn page upside down for answer.

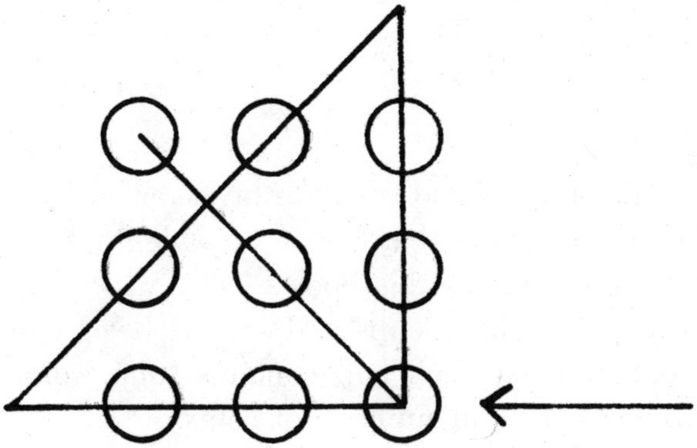

That's Certainly Odd!

People like to think they are too smart to be taken in by a trick. The odds are, though, that you'll be able to trick some people with any trick in this book.

Place ten coins beside three cups and say, "I bet I can arrange these coins so that each cup contains some coins and each cup contains an odd number of coins."

When someone shows interest in the dare you can add fuel to the fire by going on to say, "I bet you can't do it."

It shouldn't take long before your victim is ready to throw in the towel. It looks like an impossible stunt. That's the point at which you are ready to win your bet.

Study the problem. Remember there is a sneaky trick to the answer. Can you see the trick and solve the problem?

Whether you can or not, the answer is upside down on this page.

Turn page upside down for answer.

Put three coins in the first cup and three in the second. Then place four coins in the third cup and set the second cup inside the third cup. The third cup now contains seven coins (four and three) and seven is an odd number.

From One Side to the Other

Warning! Look ahead. Plan your moves. Don't fall into a trap. With those words to guide you, this stunt should not prove to be impossible. Hard, yes, but never impossible.

You need six coins. Pennies are fine unless you are well off and can afford dimes. Place three coins heads up in spaces 1, 2, and 3. Leave space 4 vacant. Place the other three coins tails up in spaces 5, 6, and 7.

The object of the contest is to move the heads into spaces 5, 6, and 7 and the tails to spaces 1, 2, and 3.

These are the rules. Heads-up coins may move only to the right. Tails-up coins move only toward the left. No coin may be moved backwards. A coin may move into the vacant space when the vacant space is next to it. A coin may jump over a coin of a different kind and land in the empty space. (A heads-up may jump a tails-up but a tails-up may not jump a tails-up.)

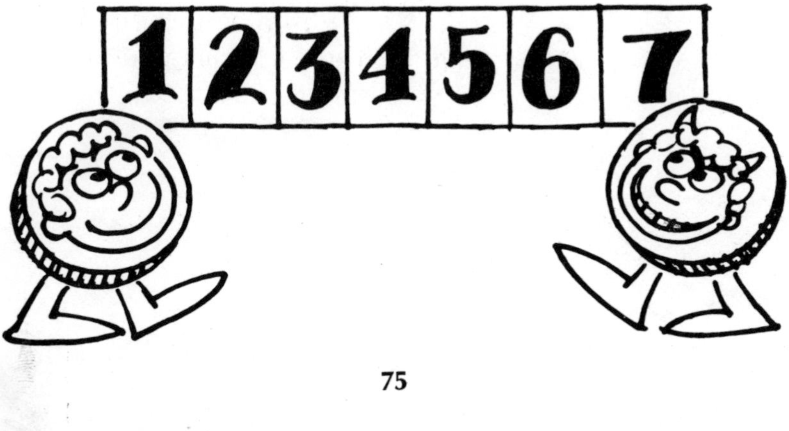

1 2 3 4 5 6 7

Work on this puzzle until you can complete it in fifteen moves. Then go looking for opponents. You might say to them, "I bet I can do this puzzle in less moves than you can." If you want to be on the safe side you might say, "I bet you can't complete this puzzle in less moves than I can." Just be sure you can do it in fifteen moves before making your challenge, of course.

Turn page upside down for answer.

Starting position: h h h o t t t (0 = space)

1. h h o h t t t
2. h h t h o t t
3. h h t h t o t
4. h h t o t h t
5. h o t h t h t
6. o h t h t h t
7. t h o h t h t
8. t h t h o h t

9. t h t h t h o
10. t h t h t o h
11. t h t o t h h
12. t o t h t h h
13. t t o h t h h
14. t t t h o h h
15. t t t o h h h

Moon Base

The nation's first base on the moon was being built at last. The first moon base consisted of six buildings. You can see the base layout on the map.

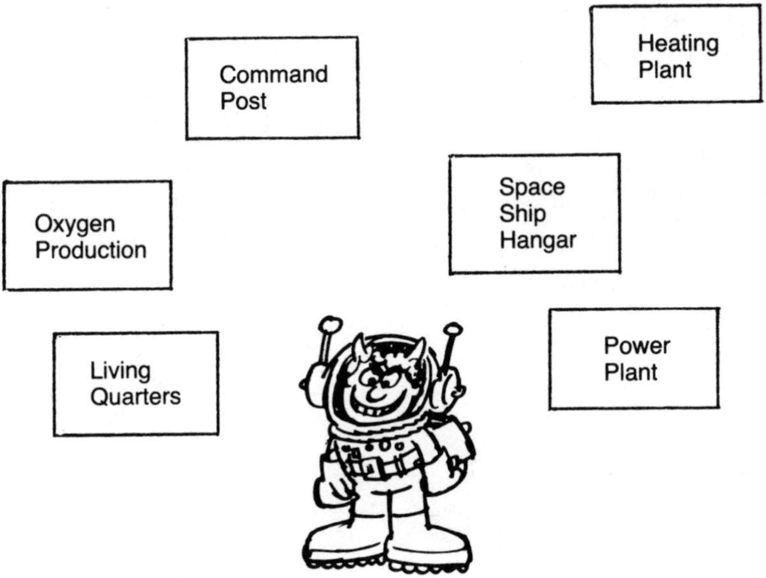

The engineers have to connect the Heating to the Command Post, the Space Ship Hangar, and to the Living Quarters. Then the Power Plant must also be connected to the Command Post, the Space Ship Hangar, and the Living Quarters. Finally, Oxygen Production must also be connected to the Command Post, the Space Ship Hangar, and the Living Quarters.

At once, the engineers run into problems. Their connecting pipes and lines may run in any direction and may be as long as needed. However, no pipe or line may cross any other pipe or line. No pipe or line may cross itself. Finally, no pipe or line may run through, under, or over another building and continue on. In other words, a pipe or line must go into a building to supply heat or power or oxygen. That pipe or line may not pass *through* the building. It must *connect to* the building and stop there.

Since there are to be only three pipes from the Heating Plant, three more from Oxygen Production, and three lines from the Power Plant, it looks like an easy job. It isn't. After weeks and months of trying, the engineers say the task is impossible. And they are correct! There is no way to set up the moon base under the conditions given.

You don't believe it is impossible. No one does. The task looks too simple to be impossible. Try it. Then try it again. Try it as many times as you wish. You will never be able to connect the final pipe or line. After you've found that it really is not possible, then spring this one on others.

Count Down

All our lives we put things in their proper order. By now, you should be an expert at putting numbers in order. Study the column of numbers below. As you can see, most of the numbers between one and fifteen are in the column. Those numbers in the column are now in their proper order. The numbers 4 and 9 are not in the column.

After you have decided why the numbers are arranged as they are, put 4 and 9 in their correct places.

8
11
15
5
14
1
7
6
10
13
3
12
2

After you have decided where to place 4 and 9, check the solution just to make certain you figured out the pattern. Then try this one on your friends. For such a plain little puzzle it fools almost everyone who tries it.

Turn page upside down for answer.

The numbers are in alphabetical order. Four should follow five and nine comes after fourteen.

What a Strange Arrangement

Place four dimes and four pennies on a table. Tell your opponent, "I bet I can arrange these eight coins so that I have two rows in which there are just two pennies in each row. There will also be six rows which each contain only two dimes. Oh, yes. There will also be four rows which have two pennies and a dime in each row."

Of course, you can do it. At least you can do it after you've worked at it for a while and then checked your answer with the upside-down answer below.

You might also dare your opponent to do the job himself or herself before you show *your* ability.

This arrangement really isn't all that difficult to see through. Just keep in mind that a row here is a straight line but that straight lines may run in a great many directions.

Turn page upside down for answer.

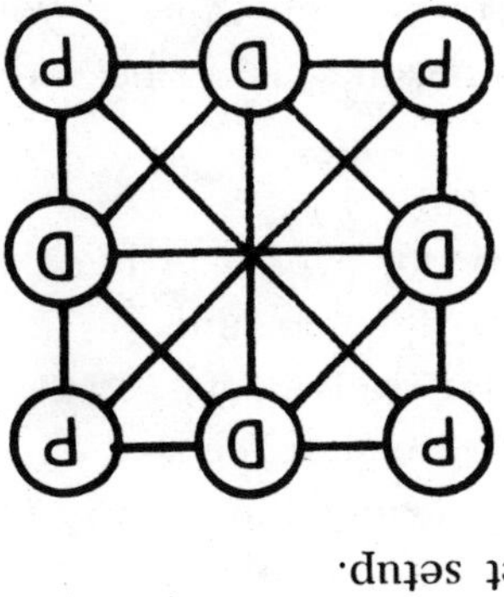

Here is the correct setup.

I Win – You Lose

Everyone likes to be a winner. With this little arithmetic game you will always be a winner, unless you play against someone who finds out how the game works.

The object of the game is for each player to write or say a number from one to six. First one says or writes a number, then the other player does. Each number given is added to the previous number or the total of the previous numbers. The player who says the number which brings the total to thirty is the winner.

Here's how the game goes.

Opponent says five.

You say four which brings the total to nine.

Opponent says three for a total of twelve.

You say four to bring the total to sixteen.

Opponent says one for a seventeen total.

You say six for a total of twenty-three.

At this point your opponent looks sick. If he says one you will say six. Should he say two you will say five. If he says three you'll say four and so on. The game is yours.

Let's run through another game just to be sure you have it well in mind.

You begin by saying two.

Your opponent says three for a total of five.

You say four to bring the total to nine.

Opponent says three for a twelve total.

You say four to make the total sixteen.

Opponent says five which brings the total to twenty-one.

You say two for a total of twenty-three.

Again your opponent is beaten. No matter what number your opponent gives from one to six, you will be able to bring the total to thirty with your next number. You win again. Lucky you!

Look back over the two games illustrated. Figure out the secret of play. Then check your idea with the solution on this page.

Once you're sure of yourself, go in search of opponents. So long as you play with care you will win far more times than you will lose.

Turn page upside down for answer.

Unbeatable totals are 9, 16, 23, and 30.

The key is 9.

If your opponent gives a 3 or larger to start you go to 9 at once. If your opponent gives a 1 or 2 to start, you give a 1. In the case of 2 + 1 = 3 you are in trouble if your opponent gives 6. Give 1 for 10 total and if your opponent gives anything lower than 6 you will still be able to get to 16.

If you start, begin with 2. Your opponent's number can't reach 9 but whatever you add can.

The only time you are in danger of losing is when your opponent begins with 1 or 2. You will only lose then if your opponent knows about 9, 16, and 23 as totals.

Draw the Answer

Here's the problem. Look closely at the drawing below for ten seconds or so.

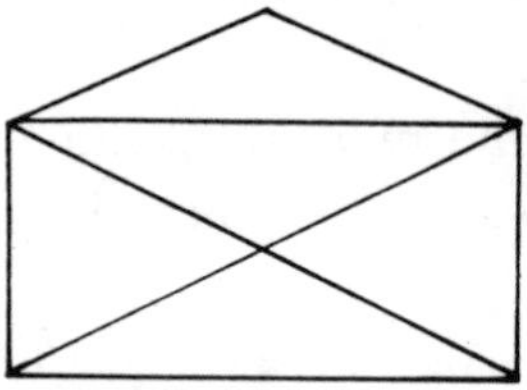

Now, take your pencil in hand and draw the figure above on another sheet of paper. Start at any point on the drawing you wish. Draw the figure as it is above without ever lifting your pencil from the paper and without going over any lines you have already drawn.

It isn't all that hard. However, not very many people do it correctly in one try. Are you one of them?

If you goof up the first time, don't peek at the answer. Try it again and again until you solve the puzzle.

Though almost everyone can do this puzzle, it is a fairly safe bet that most people won't finish it correctly on their first try.

Turn page upside down for answer.

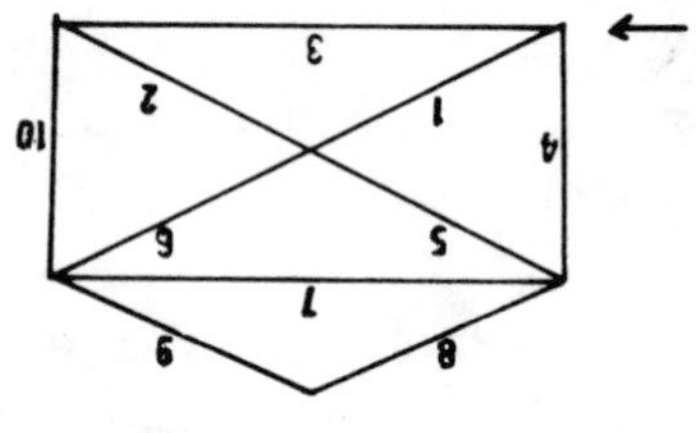

Invert and Escape

Arrange four pencils and an eraser on a table so they form the outline of a glass as shown. Toothpicks work fine, also.

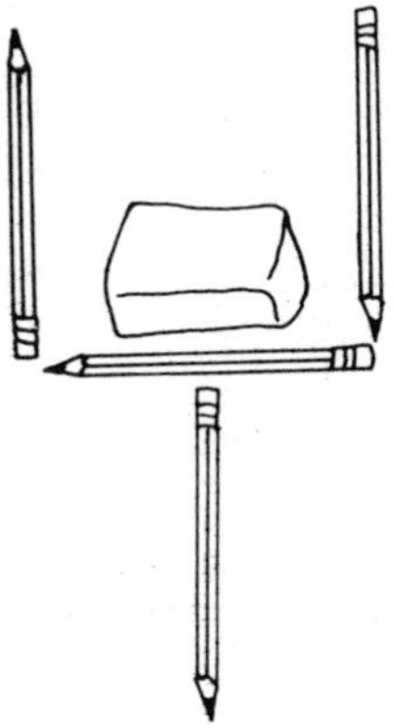

Make your bet when you say that by moving just two of the pencils you will not only turn the outline of the glass upside down but you'll let the eraser escape from the glass at the same time. Promise that when you turn the glass over, it will have the same shape it now has.

Let your opponents try this on their own a time or two to decide whether they will take your bet or not. For that matter, try it by yourself now. Can you win your own bet?

Check the answer when you either think you have solved the problem or when you have given up. It is really very easy.

Turn page upside down for answer.

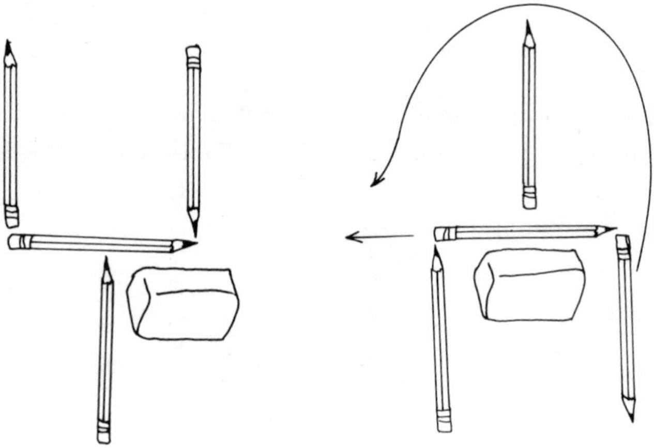

Move the two pencils as shown by the arrows.

Matches and Toothpicks

In the days when people used wooden matches to light stoves and fireplaces, puzzles of this sort were called matchstick problems. Toothpicks are more practical, today. For that matter, pencil and paper and a good eraser will do the job with a whole lot less fuss and bother.

The object in puzzles of this sort is to change one figure to a new figure by moving or removing one or more matches, toothpicks, or lines. We'll begin with a simple one to get you going.

Set up the figure below from toothpicks or lines drawn on a piece of paper. This is the dare. Take away only one toothpick or line so that the figure then contains only three squares.

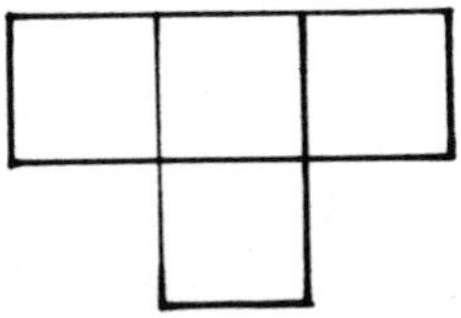

As you do these puzzles and later when you dare others to do them, keep this in mind. A square has four sides equal in length. A rectangle may have two short and two long sides. Don't try to claim an answer, which does not have squares but has rectangles instead. And don't leave a line hanging in space. Every solution must form perfect squares. No loose lines are allowed.

With all this in mind, here's a second problem. Take away six sides so that only two squares are left. Here's a hint. Squares come in many sizes.

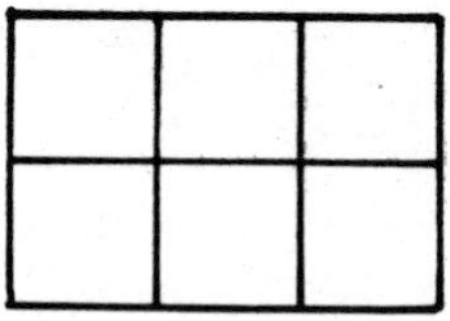

Now try this. Remove eight matches or toothpicks and leave four squares behind.

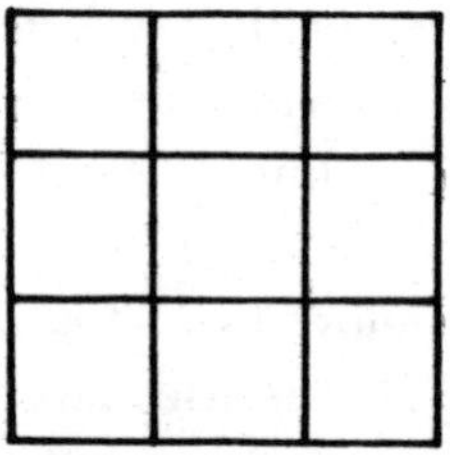

Next, take away six matches or marks so that only three squares remain in the figure.

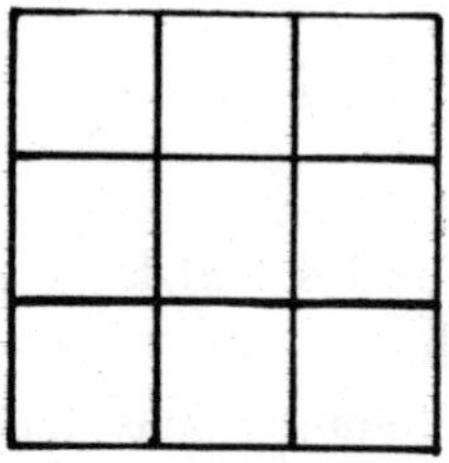

With this last problem you will be moving matches or sides instead of taking them away from the figure. Move three matches to new locations so the new figure will contain four squares.

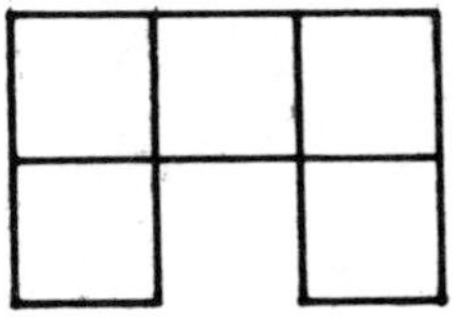

After checking your answers with the ones that are upside down you should be ready to present these puzzles to your friends. You might also enjoy making some match and toothpick challenges of your own. The five here are only a few possible puzzles. There are many more waiting for you to find them.

Turn page upside down for answer.

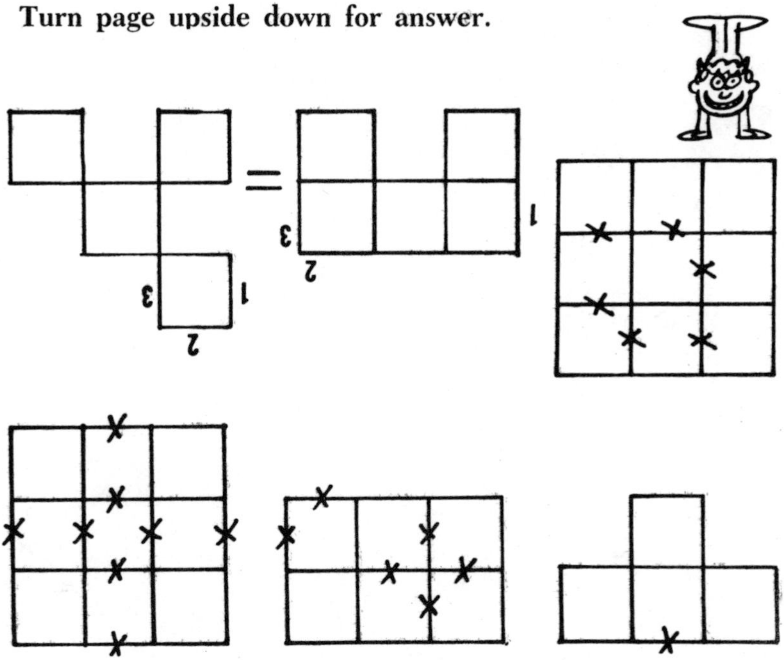

The side to be removed is marked with an x.

LISTEN AS YOU LOOK

What's Next?

Everyone knows how to count. Here is a listening stunt, which puts a person's counting skill to a quick test.

Have someone tell you what number comes next or follows each number you say. Be sure to tell the person to answer quickly. This, of course, keeps them from having enough time to stop and think.

Begin by saying, "19."

Naturally, your opponent will answer, "20."

Then you say, "186."

Next say, "294."

Then say, "567."

Go on to say, "1026."

Say next, "2169."

Then say, "4099."

Here is where you win or lose. If you have kept saying numbers rapidly, the chances are that the person you are playing against will say, "5000" when you say, "4099," instead of 4100. Try this with a few people and see if this isn't the case.

You do not need to memorize the numbers given above. Just start with small numbers and work up to larger ones. Be sure that the final number you use is 4099, or 5099, or 6099, and so forth.

Reading Lesson

Reading is one of the most important of all skills. This quick problem will test your skill in reading. Read the following proverb from Ben Franklin.

EARLY TO BED
AND EARLY TO
TO RISE MAKES
A MAN HEALTHY,
WEALTHY, AND WISE

Did you read the proverb exactly as it is written here? Read it again to make sure. Then, just to be on the safe side, check the upside-down answer.

This is an excellent little problem to present to others. Type Franklin's proverb on a card or piece of paper or print it in block letters exactly as above. Ask your victim to read aloud exactly what is there. Most people will find they need a bit of help with their reading after they take your reading test.

Turn page upside down for answer.

Look at lines two and three. They read, and EARLY TO TO RISE. There is an extra "to" in the proverb.

Little Red Firetruck

Here is a little spoken puzzle which really makes people wonder whether or not they are losing their minds. Ask your victim to repeat exactly what you say. Then begin.

Say, "Little red firetruck."

Naturally, your victim says, "Little red firetruck."

Next say, "Little red, blue, red firetruck."

Most people will repeat, "Little red, blue, red firetruck."

Grin, shake your head, and say quickly, "See, I knew you couldn't do it!"

At that point your victim probably will look puzzled and ask for you to do it again. If he or she doesn't, you might suggest taking another crack at it.

Then, do as before.

Say, "Little red firetruck." Then say, "Little red, blue, red firetruck."

Then, as before, shake your head and say something like, "You messed up again!" or "You still haven't got it right!"

Of course, the trick is that your victim must repeat what you say the third time. This may be, "See, I knew you couldn't do it!" or "You messed up again!" or whatever it is you said.

It is amazing how many people you can trick time after time with this little puzzle.

The Joke's on Me

Everyone knows someone who is just too smart to be real. That person knows every answer, remembers everything, and spells like a whiz. Here's your chance to bring that person down to size.

Tell your victim you are going to give him or her a few words to pronounce. Be sure the person understands that all he or she has to do is just say the word.

Begin by saying, "What does s-m-o-k-e spell?"

Of course, the answer is "smoke."

Now ask, "What does j-o-k-e spell?"

And, naturally, the answer will be "joke."

Now ask, "What does f-o-l-k spell?"

Your victim will tell you that spells "folk."

Then say, "What is the white of an egg?"

Unless your victim is a lot more careful than most people, the answer will be "yolk."

When that happens it is time for you to look superior. You can say something like, "The yolk is the yellow part of the egg. I asked you about the white of the egg." And, of course, the joke is on your victim.

If your victim is really a genius, he or she will tell you the white of an egg is the albumen. If that happens, then the joke is actually on you for trying this stunt with an egghead!

With Both Eyes Open

Here's a little trick which will work for you more times than it won't.

Begin by telling your listeners that you have certain magic powers. Say that you have found that you have the power to cause other people to open their eyes without touching them. Stress that you are able to do this just by speaking certain magic words to them when they have their eyes closed.

"I bet I can do this to you," you dare.

Once your bet has been accepted, it's all up to you.

Mutter a few magic words and phrases while looking your partner in the eye. Then say, "Now, close your eyes."

The instant your opponent closes his or her eyes you command sharply, "No, not that way. You've done it all wrong!"

At this point most people automatically open their eyes in order to find out what they did wrong. When they do, you've won your bet.

But what if they don't fall for your trick and keep their eyes closed? Then you've just lost a bet. Win a few—lose a few. Sorry about that.

A Room for the Night

Before presenting this listening problem to your friends it will be fun for you to read it through and try to solve it on your own.

Here's the way the story goes. Three fellows arrived at a bargain hotel. The clerk charged them $10.00 each for the night since they were all going to share one large room. After the clerk collected $30.00 he realized he should only have charged the men $25.00 for their room. He called for the bellhop and told him to take $5.00 back to the men.

The bellhop didn't know how to divide $5.00 into three equal parts so he gave $1.00 each back to the men. The other $2.00 he kept for himself. The men got back $1.00 each. This meant they had each paid $9.00 for the room. Three men paying $9.00 each makes a total of $27.00 they paid for the room since three times nine is twenty-seven. The bellhop has $2.00. Twenty-seven plus two equals $29.00. What happened to the missing dollar?

Work on this until you know what happened to the other dollar. Check the solution and then go looking for some friends you wish to confuse when you tell them, "I bet you can't tell me what's wrong in this little story."

Turn page upside down for answer.

The money is all there. The clerk still has $25.00. The bellhop has $2.00 and the men in the room have $3.00. It is all in the way the problem is stated. Looking at it another way, the men have now paid $27.00 for the room. Of that amount the clerk has $25.00 and the bellhop has $2.00.

Grandmother Does Not Like Tea

Before you are ready to go out and puzzle others with this listening game, it might be a good idea for you to figure out for yourself just what grandmother does and does not like.

For example, grandmother likes milk but does not like buttermilk.

She likes cheese but hates cottage cheese.

She loves spinach and does not like lettuce.

Grandmother is fond of celery but dislikes beets.

She goes for oranges but does not eat grapefruit.

Grandmother enjoys cabbage but dislikes turnips.

She is fond of her nephews but does not care for her brothers.

Grandmother likes her grandsons but does not care for her granddaughters.

She likes purple but dislikes violet.

Wednesday is fine but Thursday is terrible.

Grandmother enjoys July and dislikes August.

By now, you should be ready to come up with some pairs of things Grandmother does and does not like. First, just to be absolutely certain you are onto the game, check the upside-down answer on this page.

Then go in search of listeners. This listening game is so simple it often drives people crazy. Especially is this so when three or four players pick up on it at once and one or two remain in the dark.

Turn page upside down for answer.

Grandmother does not like any word or name with the letter *t* in it.

Look Sharply

Believe it or not, their are five errers in this short paragraph. Study the paragraph carefully. Feel free to reed it as many times as necessary. Don't give up to easily. Keep at it until you find all of them.

An answer is given below if you can't locate all five.

This is another of those great dares to present to the wise guy who knows everything. Just say, "I bet you can't find the five things wrong with this paragraph." Your victim can't help but accept a dare like that.

Turn page upside down for answer.

There is written as "their." Errors is spelled "errers." Read is written "reed." The to used should be "too." The fifth error, and the hard one to spot, is that the paragraph only contains four errors, not five.

Think Fast!

It is surprising how many people get scared when they are asked to do something simple in a certain amount of time. Faced with the time limit, lots of people do even simple things quite poorly.

Tell your victim that you're willing to bet he or she can't name ten parts of the body within thirty seconds. Before your victim begins to rattle off names, be sure he or she understands the total dare.

"There are at least eleven body parts, which are spelled using three letters, and which are not slang expressions. I bet you can't name ten of them in thirty seconds. In fact, I'm so certain, I'll even give you the word 'leg' to get you started. Ready, set, go. Hurry, because I'm timing you."

Try this one yourself. Can you name ten three-letter body parts in half a minute? Bet you can't!

Turn page upside down for answer.

Leg, toe, hip, rib, arm, eye, ear, lip, gum, jaw, fat.

What a Shot!

The archery target shown on this page isn't the everyday target used in archery class. But it is a target which should help you win a bet or two.

Here's your dare. You are willing to bet that an archer can shoot six arrows into the target and get a score of exactly one hundred. None of the six arrows will miss the target. All will hit one of the scoring rings shown. And the score will be exactly one hundred.

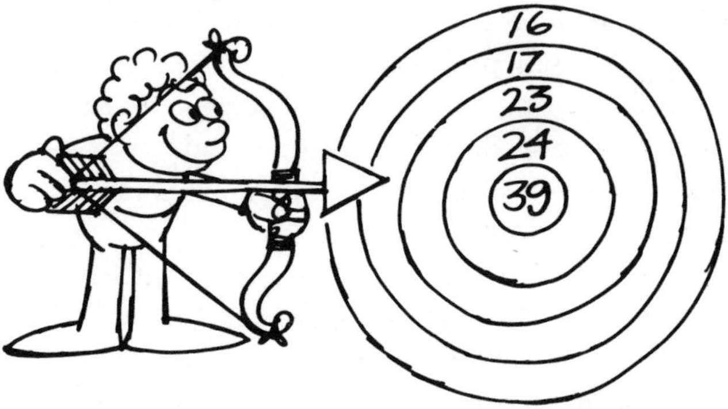

Can you win your own bet now? Don't be too quick to check the upside-down answer. This one is a bit hard to see, but it is possible.

Turn page upside down for answer.

Try two arrows in the 16 ring and four in the 17 ring.

Spelling Can Be Hard

Find an opponent who is a fairly good speller. Dare that person to spell three words correctly aloud. Stress the fact that he or she may make only one attempt to spell each word.

Once the dare has been accepted, you are ready to begin.

Tell your victim, "Spell receive."

He or she will probably spell out, "R e c e i v e."

"Now spell neighbor," you continue.

The answer will probably be "N e i g h b o r."

At this point you say in a firm voice, "Wrong."

Your friend will doubtless protest and say something to the effect, "N e i g h b o r spells neighbor."

Again you say, "Wrong."

This goes on and on until your victim either catches on to the fact he or she was supposed to spell "wrong" or until you finally let a very frustrated person in on the trick.

Or, you can pretend to be willing to let your victim try again and go through a second set of words. Naturally, after the second spelling you'll say, "Wrong," and the whole cycle begins again.

Count the Rectangles

When you bet someone they can't correctly count the number of rectangles in the figure below they are likely to accept your bet.

Remind your victim that all squares are rectangles and that rectangles come in a variety of sizes. So, two squares next to each other form a rectangle in this figure. Do three squares in a line. For that matter, a rectangle which is two squares by three squares can be found in several locations in the figure. And don't forget overlapping rectangles.

Try this one first before daring others to count the rectangles.

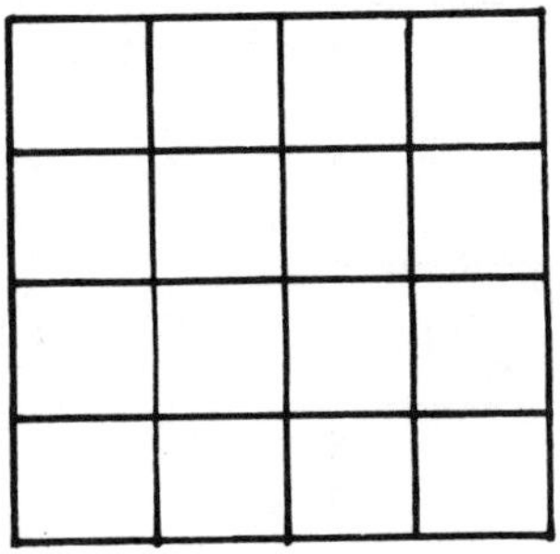

Here's a hint. Set up a list of all the possible rectangles in the figure. Count all the rectangles of each size and record that number. Do one size at a time. Don't be too quick to think you've counted all the rectangles.

The upside-down answer on the next page indicates there are quite a few hidden in the figure.

Turn page upside down for answer.

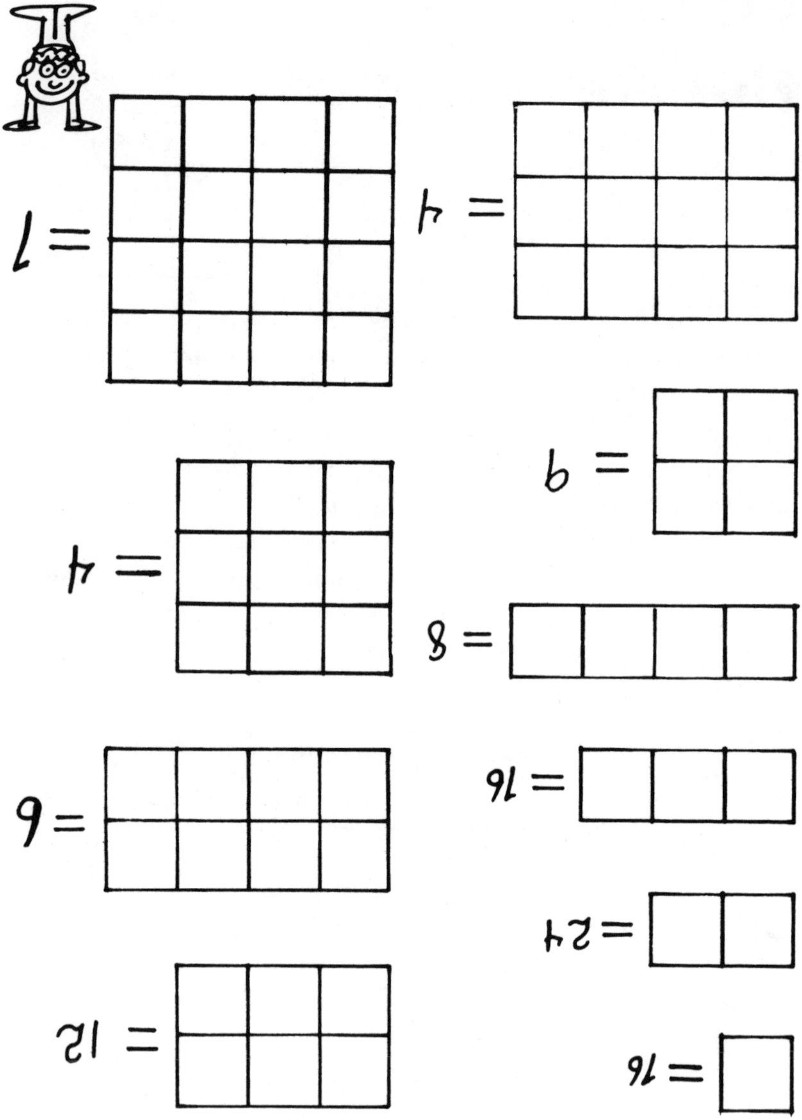

There are 100 rectangles in the figure.

Mind Reader

You might like to set the stage for this stunt by telling a friend you have discovered how to read minds. Naturally, your friend probably won't believe this. When that happens, you are ready to prove your point.

Tell your friend (really your victim) to hold some coins in his or her hands. In one hand, hold an odd number of coins. In the other hand, hold an even number of coins. (Pebbles or bits of paper will work just as well as coins.)

Be sure your friend does not tell you how many coins are being held. Once your friend has an even number of coins in one hand and an odd number of coins in the other, have your friend do a little arithmetic.

Have him multiply the number of coins in the right hand by two. Then he should multiply the number of coins in the left hand by three, add the two totals together, and tell you their sum.

At this point you can tell your friend you did some mind reading while he did the multiplying. If the sum you were given is an even number you tell your friend he is holding an even number of coins in his left hand. When you are given an odd number as the sum you tell your friend the right hand holds an even number of coins.

Try this by yourself a few times to see how it works. Then you are all set to show off your mind-reading ability to your friends.

The reason this stunt has to work correctly is explained in the upside-down answer.

Turn page upside down for answer.

This is based on the mathematic principle that an even number multiplied by an even number results in an even product. An odd number times an even gives an even product. Only an odd number times an odd number has an odd number for a product. Therefore, an odd number from your friend indicates an odd number of coins in his or her left hand.

Ride the Bus

In city after city all over the world people are being urged to ride the bus and save gasoline. Read this paragraph about riding the bus. Be ready to answer a question when you finish reading the paragraph.

Fred started his bus route yesterday morning by stopping at Hill Street where five people got onto Fred's bus. When Fred stopped at Center Street, nine more people got onto the bus. At the Main Street stop, four people got on but six people got off Fred's bus. When Fred stopped at Lincoln Avenue, two people left the bus and only one woman got onto the bus. At the Grant Avenue stop two people got on and four got off. When Fred stopped at Washington Place, six people were waiting to get on and three wanted to get off.

Now for the question. How many stops did the bus make in the paragraph you just read?

If you knew the proper answer without looking back you are much more clever than are most people. Most people suspect they will be asked how many people are now on the bus, or how many people have gotten off. Therefore, they spend their time trying to keep track of who got on and who got off. Few people have any idea how many stops Fred's bus made.

Use either this story or make up one like it to try on your friends. Tell it fairly quickly and say very clearly the numbers of people getting on and off. Then ask how many stops the bus made. You'll be able to catch a lot of listeners with this story.

Put on Your Thinking Cap

You don't have to be a great mathematician in order to come up with the answer to this poser. In spite of this, lots and lots of people don't see how to arrive at the proper answer.

The average human head contains around 125,000 hairs. Absolutely no human head contains as many as 499,999 hairs.

A huge open-air concert was held. Exactly 500,000 people attended. No one who came to the concert was totally bald. Is it possible that no two people attending the concert had exactly the same number of hairs on their heads?

See if your answer matches the upside-down one before giving this little problem to others.

Turn page upside down for answer.

It is not possible that no two people had the same numbers of hairs on their heads. If no head ever has as many as 499,999 hairs and 500,000 people were present, one (and very likely many) pair of people had to have the same number of hairs, since every possible number of hairs from 1 to 499,999 is covered.

You Can Read My Mind

Instead of betting you can read someone else's mind, it's time to bet someone else can read yours.

Give this silly little stunt a bit of a build-up by saying you've discovered that it is sometimes possible to think very hard about a word or a phrase and cause others to be able to read your mind. After you've gotten the interest of the others, it is time to spring your trap.

"I'm willing to bet you can read my mind," you tell someone in the group. "Let's just see whether or not I'm right."

Then take a piece of paper and a pencil and turn your back on the person you have chosen. Carefully write a word on the paper. Turn back to the one who is to read your mind and fold the paper carefully two or three times.

Then ask, "Did you see what I just wrote on this paper?"

When the mind reader says, "No," it's time for you to really go into your act.

Act pleased, delighted, tell the mind reader how smart he or she is, and whatever else seems in order. Unfold the paper and show everyone that you had indeed written "No" on the folded paper.

Obviously, your friend must have read your mind.

I Doubt That

This quick little stumper will win more often than it will lose, even though some people will see through the trick and make a loser out of you.

Without showing your opponent what coins you have, put two coins in your hand. Shake them around a bit. Then, with your fist closed around the pair of coins, show your hand to your opponent.

"I've got two coins in my hand," you say. "Together they total fifteen cents. One of the coins is not a dime. I bet you can't tell me what two coins I have in my hand."

If a person doesn't see through this trick at once, it becomes almost impossible to figure out.

Can you see how it works?

Check the upside-down answer just to be on the safe side. Then find a friend to try this with.

Turn page upside down for answer.

You hold a dime and a nickel. You said one of the coins was not a dime. One wasn't. It was a nickel. The other was a dime.

Shoot for the Moon

Be certain you know how this listening game goes before you try it on your friends.

The game's object is easy enough. Each player is to make a statement in which the player names two closely related things. One of the things is correct, the other is wrong.

For example, "I like to shoot but don't want to go hunting."

The moon is great but Neptune isn't all that hot.

Scissors are fine for cutting but a knife isn't.

Butter is good but margarine is lacking in taste.

Coffee is great but hot chocolate isn't my favorite.

Books are fun to read but magazines bore me.

Doors are important but windows are silly.

Fools are fun but clowns are a waste of my time.

School is the place to be because it is more fun than being at home.

I'd rather live in a village than in a town.

Deer are pretty animals but elk are too large.

By now you should be able to shoot for the moon with some pairs of your own. If you're in doubt, or just to check yourself, give the solution a glance. Then, go looking for others who think they are pretty good listeners. This stunt often stumps even the sharpest people for quite some time.

Turn page upside down for answer.

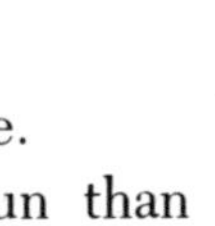

Correct answers all contain double letters.

Beauty without Brains

The easiest tricks often catch the most people. This one should do just that.

Dare someone by saying, "I bet you can't say beauty without brains three times."

Chances are your victim will say, "Beauty without brains, beauty without brains, beauty without brains."

At that point you smile and tell your victim he or she just lost the bet.

"I told you to say beauty without brains," you tell them.

When they try it again, victims will say, "Beauty without brains, beauty without brains, beauty without brains."

And again you can tell your opponent that he or she failed again.

Some people soon see through the trick and finally say, "Beauty, beauty, beauty." Some people never figure this one out and continue to repeat their error each time they try the trick.

Say What?

All spoken dares depend largely upon how well you play your part. This is no exception.

Tell your victim you can get him or her to say the word "black."

If your dare is accepted, remember to set the ground rule that each question you ask must be answered. Once this is agreed on, you're ready to do your stuff.

You might go about it something like this.

"What is the opposite of white?"

Your opponent will give some answer which is not black, of course.

"What is the darkest color?"

You'll get another answer.

"What is the color of a truck tire?"

Still another answer which is not black.

"What color is a normal typewriter ribbon?"

Yet another answer, but not black.

"What color is a tar highway?"

And yet another answer.

Continue for another few questions and answers. Immediately after getting an answer, let your face light up. Smile, look pleased, and tell your opponent. "You lose. I told you I'd get you to say _____ ." In place of _____ put in whatever the person's last answer was. If their last answer was "red" you'd say, "I told you I'd get you to say red. You lose."

At this point most people will protest immediately saying something such as, "You said I'd say black." Or, "It was black I was supposed to say."

However they say it, your opponents will almost always fall for this trick.

Of course you don't have to use "black" as the forbidden word. Any color, a number, a person's name, and such, will work just as well.

Checkerboard Squares

Who hasn't played checkers or at least looked at a checkerboard? But how many people have ever tried to count all the squares on a checkerboard? Few have. Fewer, still, have counted correctly.

As you may already know, a checkerboard has eight squares on a side. Since eight times eight equals sixty-four, then there must be sixty-four squares on a checkerboard. Wrong.

The entire board is a square, so that adds at least one more. And what about all the squares within the board which are formed when you consider two-by-two squares to make a larger square. And how about the three by three squares and those four by four, and so on. And don't forget that the larger squares may overlap one another.

Begin by counting the number of squares for yourself. Don't be too quick to check the upside-down answer below. Work this out by yourself and then rework it just to be on the safe side. Then you can check your answer with the one given. Be sure you can see how to locate all the squares given in the solution. And be sure you count just squares, not rectangles which aren't squares.

Once you're positive you can locate all those illusive squares it is time to dare some unsuspecting friend to count all the squares on the checkerboard. Very few people arrive at the right number on the first try.

Turn page upside down for answer.

There are 204 squares on the checkerboard:

1 × 1 = 64	2 × 2 = 49	3 × 3 = 36
4 × 4 = 25	5 × 5 = 16	6 × 6 = 9
7 × 7 = 4	8 × 8 = 1	

Note that all the totals (64, 49, 36, etc.) are square numbers.

You've Got to Be Kidding

To make this stunt work you have to find a sucker. You have to be willing to use a little trickery, as well.

Have the person you've chosen as the sucker take a coin from pocket or purse. Tell the person to look closely at the date on the coin but not to tell you the date.

Next, instruct your victim to place the coin in the palm of your hand with the date down. This leaves you looking at the tail side of the coin.

Stare hard and long at the tail of the coin. Then look the poor victim in the eye and say, "I have special powers. Just by looking at this coin I can tell you the date. Do you want to bet I can't?"

Most people will want to know whether you are going to turn the coin over or drop it or any of a number of tricky things. You can honestly tell them you aren't. "I'm going to tell you the date and all I have to do is to continue to look at the tail side of the coin," is your answer.

When your bet is accepted you simply tell your victim the current day's date. After all, you never said you would tell the date on the coin. You only said you'd be able to tell the date.

Tricky, isn't it?

A Quick Conclusion

What better way to end this book than with a trio of quick bets which will quite often catch others off guard. Here's a hint, though. Use only one of these per person.

Quick Bet 1. "I'll bet I can tell you a word almost everyone pronounces incorrectly."

Quick Bet 2. "I bet I know a word which little children and old adults all say wrong every time they use it."

Quick Bet 3. "I bet I know of a word that you and I both pronounce correctly each time we speak it."

You should be sharp enough by now to see through these quickies. If you need to check yourself, just read the upside-down answer.

Turn page upside down for answer.

Bet 1. Incorrectly
Bet 2. Wrong
Bet 3. Correctly

INDEX